WIND POWER

A TRUE BOOK®
by
Christine Petersen

Children's Press®
A Division of Scholastic Inc.

New York Toronto London Auckland Sydney
Mexico City New Delhi Hong Kong
Danbury, Connecticut

C1

Reading Consultant
Jeanne Clidas
*State University of
New York College*

Content Consultant
Tony Rogers
*Renewable Energy Research
Laboratory,
University of Massachusetts*

These old windmills on the
Greek island of Rhodes were
once used to grind grain.

Library of Congress Cataloging-in-Publication Data

Petersen, Christine
    Wind power / by Christine Petersen.
        p. cm. — (A true book)
Summary: Describes how wind occurs in nature and how it can be used
to produce electricity, both now and in the future.
Includes bibliographical references and index.
    ISBN 0-516-22809-9 (lib. bdg.)   0-516-21943-X (pbk.)
    1. Wind power plants—Juvenile literature. [1. Wind power.] I. Title.
II. Series.
TK1541.P48 2004
621.31'2136—dc21

                                                            2003006383

1 2 3 4 5 6 7 8 9 10 R 13 12 11 10 09 08 07 06 05 04

Contents

A breeze blows laundry on a clothesline.

What Makes the Wind Blow?

Everyone knows the wind. Even with our eyes closed, we recognize the rustling sound a breeze makes as it moves through the trees. In winter, the wind may carry an icy bite that cuts through even our thickest clothes. We watch in

delight as the wind picks up fallen leaves in autumn, spinning them across sidewalks and streets. On blustery spring days, wind tousles our hair and turns our umbrellas inside out.

But where does wind come from?

It all begins with the Sun. During the day, heat from the Sun pours onto Earth's surface. Land absorbs the heat, while water reflects most of the Sun's rays back into the air. As the air warms, it becomes lighter and rises up into the atmosphere (the "bubble" of air that surrounds the planet). Heavier cool air from nearby is sucked in along

The Sun is the primary source of wind on Earth.

the ground to fill the void. The movement of this cooler air is what we feel as wind.

Worldwide wind patterns (global winds) start at the

equator, halfway between the North and South Poles. The equator always faces the Sun, so it stays hot all year. Hot air from this region rises high into the atmosphere and drifts away from the equator.

After traveling thousands of miles north or south, the air begins to cool. It sinks and spreads outward over Earth's surface. Some of the air moves back toward the equator—this movement produces steady trade winds. The remaining cool air moves toward the poles. These winds are known as the prevailing westerlies because they travel from west to east. At the same time, cold air from the poles flows toward the equator. Because polar winds flow in a curving pattern from east to west, they are known as easterlies. Together, trade winds, westerlies, and easterlies circle the globe and cause many of Earth's weather patterns.

Local Winds

Winds change speed and direction from day to day. Many of these differences are caused by weather. Winds also shift as you move from place to place. These are known as local winds, and are often caused by changes in the shape of the land. Over wide-open plains or

Wind blows fast and strong across the prairie because there is nothing to block its path.

water, winds can blow strong and fast in a straight line. Uneven ground blocks the path of the wind, causing it to slow down and change direction often. Airplanes experience the effects of these "rough patches" as turbulence, which causes the plane to rise and fall as if it were traveling on a very bumpy road.

Local winds also occur because some parts of Earth's surface warm up more quickly than others or retain heat longer. For example, mountain slopes warm up faster than valleys (low-lying areas between mountains or hills) because sunlight reaches

A valley wind flows up the surrounding mountain slopes during the day, then changes direction at night.

them first. Warm air is light, so it rises up the slopes. Cold air rushes in at the mountain's base, causing winds to sweep through the valley. The wind changes direction at night because after the Sun sets, mountain slopes cool quickly. Warm air is pushed out of the way as cool air sinks, causing winds that flow downslope into valleys.

A similar principle applies on the seashore. Here, winds change direction every morning and evening because land and water heat up in opposite ways. By day the land warms quickly, sucking winds

The windy seashore is perfect for flying kites.

off the water. Water heats up slowly but stays warm longer at night, so winds shift after sunset, blowing from the land toward the sea.

Rivers of Air

This picture of a jet stream was taken from the *Gemini 12* spacecraft.

The highest-flying winds of all, called **jet streams,** blow far above Earth's surface where there is nothing to block their path. Jet streams form more than 5.6 miles (9 kilometers) up in the atmosphere. These massive "rivers" of air move at speeds of about 57 miles (92 km) per hour or faster, pulling air around the planet and carrying weather systems with them.

Discovering Wind Power

Many of history's most power-ful cities were built beside large rivers or near the seashore. Boats allowed ancient people to fish far offshore, trade goods with distant nations, and carry troops for war.

The first boats were simple rafts and canoes moved by

manpower, using poles and oars. But 7,000 years ago, Egyptians boating along the Nile River made a brilliant discovery. They learned that wind could push their boats from place to place. The addition of sails made it possible for boats to skim the surface of the water at great speeds and cover long distances quickly.

Over the centuries, people invented other ways to use the **energy** of the wind. Windmills were first used in China and Persia (now Iran) about 2,200 years ago, and by A.D. 1100 they were common across Asia, the Middle East, and Europe. These large machines made life easier by using the wind to

The windmill was one of the first large-scale inventions designed to make people's workloads easier.

do backbreaking work such as grinding grain, pumping water, and sawing wood.

Just as gasoline is the fuel that runs a car, wind provides power to windmills. An old-fashioned windmill looked like a tower with a pinwheel-shaped set of blades, or "sails," attached to a wheel near the top. Wind pushed against the sails, causing the wheel to spin. The spinning sails rotated a metal pole, called the shaft, which extended from the wheel down through the middle of the tower. In grain mills, the shaft turned a heavy millstone that crushed wheat, barley, and other grains into flour. Sawmills used the motion of the shaft to run a saw, which slid up and down to slice rough logs into tidy pieces of lumber.

Wind-powered grain mills and sawmills were replaced by more efficient machinery in the early 1900s. But windmills haven't gone completely out of style. Some farmers still use water-pumping windmills to drain flooded areas and to pull up underground water for irrigating crops.

Historically, windmills on farms were used to pull up underground water for irrigating crops, as well as to supply households and livestock.

High-powered windmills, called wind **turbine generators,** are used to make electricity.

Generating Electricity

Power plant workers inspect a turbine.

Like windmills, turbines are fan-shaped machines with blades that rotate when something pushes against them. (Usually that "something" is steam, wind, or flowing water.) A metal shaft connects the turbine to a generator, which is a magnet surrounded by coils of wire. The turbine rotates the shaft, and this causes the generator magnet to spin.

Large generators spin to produce electricity.

Electricity made by the spinning magnet flows into wires and is carried away from the generator, providing power to homes and industries.

The electricity is then "carried" to customers by way of power cables. The cables are usually made of copper or aluminum.

Harnessing the Wind

In the United States, about 88 percent of all electricity is made using **fossil fuels**—oil, coal, or natural gas—which formed millions of years ago from the decaying bodies of plants and animals. But fossil fuels exist only in small amounts on our planet, and supplies are being

Fossil fuels—oil (left), coal (middle), and natural gas (right)—were made over millions of years. Our supply of these resources is being used up faster than it can be replaced.

used up quickly. Fortunately, there are other sources of energy, including the wind. Wind is a **renewable resource**—it is constantly recycled in nature.

We can make all the electricity we need from it and never run out of fuel.

Harnessing the wind to make electricity is not a new idea. People in Denmark have used wind turbine generators since the 1890s, and wind-powered

Windmills are a common sight in Denmark. The country has a long tradition of using wind as an energy source.

electricity was common in the United States until the 1940s. After World War II, fossil fuels became so inexpensive that wind and other alternative fuels were nearly forgotten.

In the 1970s, an oil and gas shortage inspired scientists to take another look at alternative fuels. Researchers learned that wind can be an excellent power source. It works best if turbines are built in places where winds blow constantly at a speed of 13 miles (21 km) per hour or

Wind turbines are perched on tall towers because winds are stronger and steadier high above the ground.

faster. (Faster winds generate more electricity.) Also, because winds are stronger and steadier high above the ground, wind turbines should be placed atop towers that are at least 100 feet (30 meters) tall.

Farming the Wind

Several types of wind turbines have been invented so far, but all share a few important mechanical parts. A rotor holds the blades, which catch the wind and spin. The rotor is mounted atop a tall tower and connected to a generator box, which makes electricity.

Cables carry electricity to a main power station, where it is sent off for use in homes and businesses.

Most modern turbines have two or three airplane propeller-shaped blades that are angled in different directions to catch the wind. "Eggbeater" turbines are named for their unusual shape, which looks like a huge, stretched-out rubber band.

"Eggbeater" turbines capture winds closer to the ground.

To make large amounts of electricity, turbines can be arranged in groups. These **wind farms** are usually found in places where local winds are strong and steady year-round. In 2001, wind farms around the world produced enough electricity for 10 million homes.

Wind Power for the Future

Wind power isn't a perfect answer to our energy needs. Turbines are expensive to build, and some people complain about the noise caused by thousands of turbines working at once. Other people are worried that wind farms use up large amounts of beautiful

Tehachapi

If you drive through the Tehachapi Pass north of Los Angeles, California, you'll see an amazing sight. Nearly 5,000 tall wind turbines blanket the hillsides of this broad valley. Tehachapi is home to traditional propeller-style turbines and "eggbeater" turbines, all spinning wildly as they capture strong winds flowing through the Mojave Desert and the foothills of the Tehachapi Mountains. Together, the turbines at Tehachapi produce more energy than any other wind power plant in the world.

Thousands of people visit Tehachapi Pass to observe the wind turbines at work.

A bald eagle in flight

open space, and that hawks, eagles, and other wild birds might be killed by flying into the whirling blades.

So why should we use wind power? The answer is simple: Wind is free. Also, no matter how much we use, more wind will always be available.

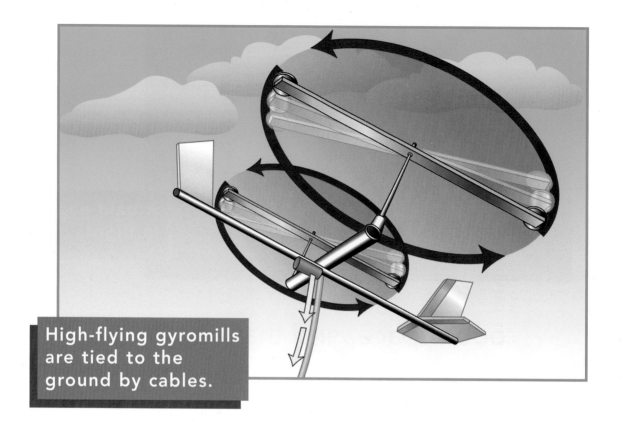

Australian scientists are among those looking for new ways to make wind power. Their idea is to use high-flying gyromills— wind turbines with wings—to capture the energy of the jet stream. Strong, steady winds from the jet stream may allow each gyromill to produce 100 times more electricity than a normal wind turbine can.

Best of all, wind power protects our environment. For example, the people of India have saved more than 3.7 million tons of coal by making electricity from wind power instead of using fossil fuels. Had that coal been burned, billions of tons of

Wind power is a clean alternative to coal-fired power stations such as this one, which emit gases produced by burning the fuel.

polluting chemicals would have poured into the air and water.

People have used renewable energy—wind, water, and sunlight—for thousands of years. Today, as fossil fuels disappear, we can once again take advantage of these natural gifts. The result will be a lasting supply of energy for people and a healthier future for the planet we call home.

The use of wind power helps preserve Earth's natural resources and beauty for our enjoyment.

To Find Out More

Here are some additional resources to help you learn more about wind power:

 **Books**

Gibson, Diane. **Wind Power.** Smart Apple Media, 2000.

Parker, Steve. **Fuels for the Future.** Raintree Steck-Vaughn, 1998.

Woelfle, Gretchen. **The Wind at Work: An Activity Guide to Windmills.** Chicago Review Press, Inc., 1997.

Woodruff, John. **Energy.** Raintree Steck-Vaughn, 1998.

Wind Energy Powers the World. (Available from Kern Wind Energy Association, P.O. Box 277, Tehachapi, CA, 93561)

Organizations and Online Sites

Wind Power
http://www.surfnetkids.com/wind.htm

This page from the Surfing the Net with Kids site contains links on wind power history, windmills and wind farms, and other wind-powered machines.

The Energy Story— Wind Energy
http://www.energyquest.ca.gov/story/chapter16.html

The California Energy Commission has compiled an exciting site just for students that includes a history of wind power and a detailed explanation of how modern wind turbines work.

The Wind: Our Fierce Friend
http://sln.fi.edu/tfi/units/energy/wind.html

Teachers and students can access a number of projects and experiments on this page from the Franklin Institute Science Museum, and link to the Web sites of other schools that study wind.

Global Wind Patterns
http://kids.earth.nasa.gov/archive/nino/global.html

This NASA Web site on weather gives an excellent, detailed description of how global winds are formed and how they move around the planet.

Learning About Renewable Energy
http://www.eere.energy.gov/erec/factsheets/rnwenrgy.html

This site from the U.S. Department of Energy provides background information on a variety of renewable energy sources, including solar, wind, and water power.

Important Words

energy the ability to do work

fossil fuels the remains of plants and animals that died millions of years ago, which can be used for fuel; includes oil, coal, and natural gas

generator a motor in which movement energy is converted to electricity

gyromills winged windmills that use jet stream winds to produce electricity

jet stream a strong current of air flowing far above Earth's surface

renewable resource a material that is naturally recycled or regrown

turbine a fan-shaped engine used to produce electricity

wind farms groups of dozens to thousands of wind turbines that produce large amounts of electricity

Index

Meet the Author

Christine Petersen is a middle-school teacher who lives near Minneapolis, Minnesota. She has also worked as a biologist for the California Academy of Sciences, the U.S. Forest Service, the U.S. Geological Survey, and the Minnesota Department of Natural Resources, studying the natural history and behavior of North American bats. In her free time, Christine enjoys snowshoeing, canoeing, birdwatching, and writing about her favorite wild animals and wild places. She is the coauthor of several True Books.